HOW TO DRAW

Amazing LETTERS

by Kathryn Clay

illustrated by Cynthia Martin

Capstone press®

Mankato, Minnesota

Snap Books are published by Capstone Press,
151 Good Counsel Drive, P.O. Box 669, Mankato, Minnesota 56002.
www.capstonepress.com

Library of Congress Cataloging-in-Publication Data
Clay, Kathryn.
    How to draw amazing letters / by Kathryn Clay; illustrated by Cynthia Martin.
    p. cm. — (Snap. Drawing fun)
    Includes bibliographical references and index.
    Summary: "Lively text and fun illustrations describe how to draw amazing letters" — Provided by publisher.
    ISBN-13: 978-1-4296-2305-6 (hardcover)
    ISBN-10: 1-4296-2305-5 (hardcover)
    1. Lettering — Technique — Juvenile literature. I. Martin, Cynthia, 1961– II. Title.
NK3600.C59 2009
745.6'1 — dc22   2008037809

Credits
Juliette Peters, designer
Abbey Fitzgerald, colorist

Photo Credits
Capstone Press/TJ Thoraldson Digital Photography, 4 (pencil), 5 (all), 32 (pencil)

The author dedicates this book to J. Smith.

1 2 3 4 5 6 14 13 12 11 10 09

Table of Contents

Getting Started

Check out a billboard, a street sign, or a book cover. Each one uses a different type of lettering, but they all have the same purpose. They want to get your attention. To do this, they use fonts in different colors and sizes. Now it's your turn to catch someone's attention. With your skills and the instructions in this book, you'll be creating cool messages in no time.

Maybe you want to make school banners? Practice drawing the All-Star ABCs. Perhaps you're planning to make homemade greeting cards? The Fancy Font adds a special touch. Would you rather design fun scrapbook pages? Create cool captions using the Daisy Crazy letters.

Of course, there are many ways to draw and design letters. Once you've mastered some of the letters in this book, you'll be able to draw your own stylish script. Let your imagination run wild, and see what kinds of amazing letters you can create.

Must-Have Materials

1. First you'll need something to draw on. Any blank, white paper will work well.

2. Pencils are a must for these drawing projects. Be sure to keep a bunch nearby.

3. Because sharp pencils make clean lines, you'll be sharpening those pencils a lot. Have a pencil sharpener handy.

4. Even the best artist needs to erase a line now and then. Pencil erasers wear out fast. A rubber or kneaded eraser will last much longer.

5. To make your drawings pop off the page, use colored pencils or markers.

Bubbles

Do you want fun-looking letters without a lot of work? Bubble letters are the ultimate design. These curvy letters are easy to make and add a whole lot of style.

Make your bubble letters stand out by filling in each letter with a different color.

STEP 1

STEP 2

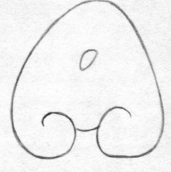

STEP 3

Big and Bold

Need an unmistakable way to get your point across? Say it loud and proud with Big and Bold letters. Fill in these big, block letters any way you'd like. The message is still clear. When people see these letters, they'll know you mean business.

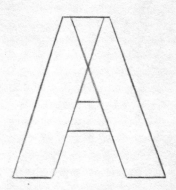

Try creating a different pattern inside each letter. Draw stars, zigzag stripes, or other fun prints.

STEP 1

STEP 2

STEP 3

ABCDEFGH
IJKLMNOPQR
STUVWXYZ

Daisy Crazy

It's been raining all day, and you've been stuck inside. Try bringing the outside in with Daisy Crazy letters. Spend the day capturing your special memories in a colorful scrapbook. Grab some favorite photos and add fun, flowery captions.

STEP 1

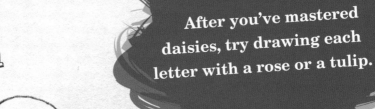

After you've mastered daisies, try drawing each letter with a rose or a tulip.

STEP 2

STEP 3

abcdefgh
ijklmnopqr
stuvwxyz

Our sleep-over

Fancy Font

You're creating a personalized message for someone special. Plain, boring letters just won't do. The Fancy Font is an elaborate alphabet that might be tricky at first. But just like mastering soccer or learning an instrument, practice makes perfect.

For a royal look, color the tips yellow. Fill in the rest of the letters with purple or red.

STEP 1

STEP 2

STEP 3

ABCDEFGH
IJKLMNOPQR
STUVWXYZ

THANK YOU

Eat Your Words

Celebrate in style with words that look good enough to eat. Use this appetizing alphabet to create your next birthday party invitations. It's a fun way to get your guests all the important info for the big event.

Use your favorite food to create a new font. Cheese and pepperoni make letters look like mini pizzas. Chocolate sauce and a cherry create hot fudge sundae letters.

STEP 1

STEP 2

STEP 3

abcdefgh
ijklmnopqr
stuvwxyz

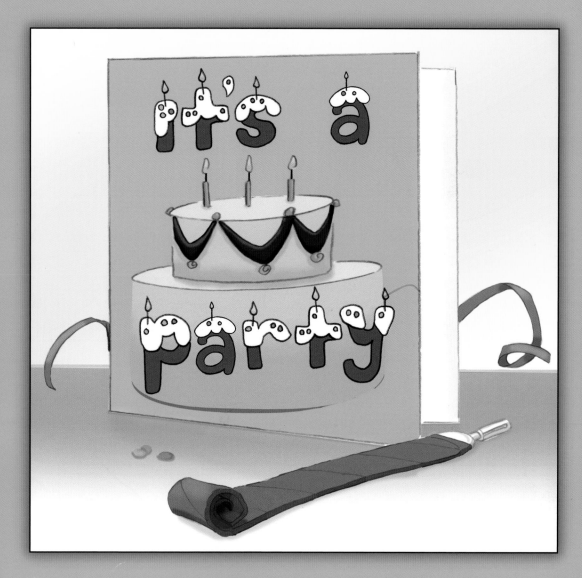

All-Star ABCs

You're planning a big event at your school. A flashy poster is a great way to get the word out. Use the All-Star ABCs to promote everything from a class carnival to an ice cream social. Then get ready for a record turnout.

To switch up this style, try replacing the stars with hearts or flowers.

STEP 1

STEP 2

STEP 3

ABCDEFGH
IJKLMNOPQR
STUVWXYZ

ENCHANTMENT UNDER THE STARS

Curly Swirls

Your writing should reflect your fun and unique personality. The curls and swirls of these letters are a great solution. Use this design when you want to show off your one-of-a-kind style.

For a fun variation, try filling in these letters with polka dots.

STEP 1

STEP 2

STEP 3

a b c d e f g h
i j k l m n o p q r
s t u v w x y z

my room

Athletic Alphabet

You don't have to be a cheerleader to show your school spirit. Just grab some poster board and a few markers. Add your message using the Athletic Alphabet. Then fill in the letters with your school colors.

Try coloring in the letters to look like basketballs, baseballs, or soccer balls.

STEP 1

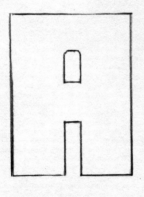

STEP 2

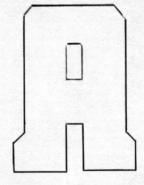

STEP 3

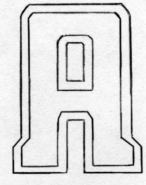

ABCDEFGH
IJKLMNOPQR
STUVWXYZ

Graffiti

Look around your neighborhood. You might notice bright, bold graffiti on signs and buildings. But drawing on buildings will get you in trouble. Instead, use this style of lettering to add a burst of color to your notebooks.

Try adding a thick, black outline around the letters to make them stand out.

STEP 1

STEP 2

STEP 3

ABCDEFGH
IJKLMNOPQR
STUVWXYZ

Holiday

Candy canes make delicious holiday treats. But did you know they also make fun letters? Use this style to create a special gift tag for your holiday presents.

Draw letters using other holiday items. Start with lights or snowflakes. Then create with your own holiday designs.

STEP 1

STEP 2

STEP 3

A B C D E F G H
I J K L M N O P Q R
S T U V W X Y Z

Superhero Script

Pow! Zap! Bang! Comic books aren't just about the pictures. Watch your words come to life with these chunky letters and starbursts. With a few extra strokes of your pen, plain text is transformed into exploding sound effects.

After you've practiced this drawing, try creating other sound effects like SPLAT! or BAM!

STEP 1

STEP 2

STEP 3

To finish this drawing, turn to the next page. ⇨

STEP 4

STEP 5

28

ABCDEFGHI
JKLMNOPQR
STUVWXYZ

Glossary

appetizing (AP-uh-tye-zing) — appealing to
someone's taste

elaborate (i-LAB-ur-it) — complicated and detailed

font (FAHNT) — a set of type of one size and style

graffiti (gruh-FEE-tee) — pictures drawn or words
written on the walls of buildings or other surfaces

personalized (PUR-suhn-a-liesd) — belonging to
a particular person

starburst (STAR-burst) — a pattern of lines from
a central object

unique (yoo-NEEK) — one of a kind

variation (vair-ee-AY-shun) — something that
is slightly different from another thing of the
same type

Hufford, Deborah. *Scrapbooking: Keep Your Memories Special.* Crafts. Mankato, Minn.: Capstone Press, 2006.

Lettering in Crazy, Cool, Quirky Style. Palo Alto, Calif.: Klutz, 2006.

Scheuer, Lauren. *Letter Art 2: Funky and Fun Letter Designs to Draw.* American Girl Library. Middleton, Wis.: Pleasant Company, 2005.

Internet Sites

FactHound offers a safe, fun way to find educator-approved Internet sites related to this book.

Here's what you do:
1. Visit *www.facthound.com*
2. Choose your grade level.
3. Begin your search.

This book's ID number is 9781429623056.

FactHound will fetch the best sites for you!

Index